Theory Paper   Grade 2   2017   A
Model Answers

1   (10)

2   (10)

3   (10)

4   (10)

harmonic

melodic

or

or

5   (10)

(a) 3rd   5th   4th   1st /   8th /   7th   3rd   6th   2nd
                                           8th / 8ve   8ve / 1st

(b) C♯

6 (10)

7 (10)

8 (10)

Con moto means:

more movement	☐
less movement	☐
without movement	☐
with movement	✔

Adagio means:

quick	☐
slow	✔
at a medium speed	☐
fairly quick	☐

non troppo means:

too much	☐
not in time	☐
very much	☐
not too much	✔

sostenuto means:

in the same way	☐
in the style of	☐
sustained	✔
expressive	☐

mf means:

very loud	☐
moderately quiet	☐
moderately loud	✔
loud	☐

⟍ means:

gradually getting louder	☐
gradually getting quieter	✔
gradually getting quicker	☐
gradually getting slower	☐

9 (a) (10)

    (i)   dotted minim / dotted half note

    (ii)   Bar 5

    (iii) C major

    (iv) true

    (v)   two

  (b)   **Adagio ma non troppo** (10)

Theory Paper   Grade 2   2017   B
Model Answers

1 (10)

2 (10)

3 (10)

4 (10)

(a)

(b) B♭ major

5 E minor   A major   D minor   (10)

C major   F major

6 (10)

harmonic

melodic

or

or

7 (10)

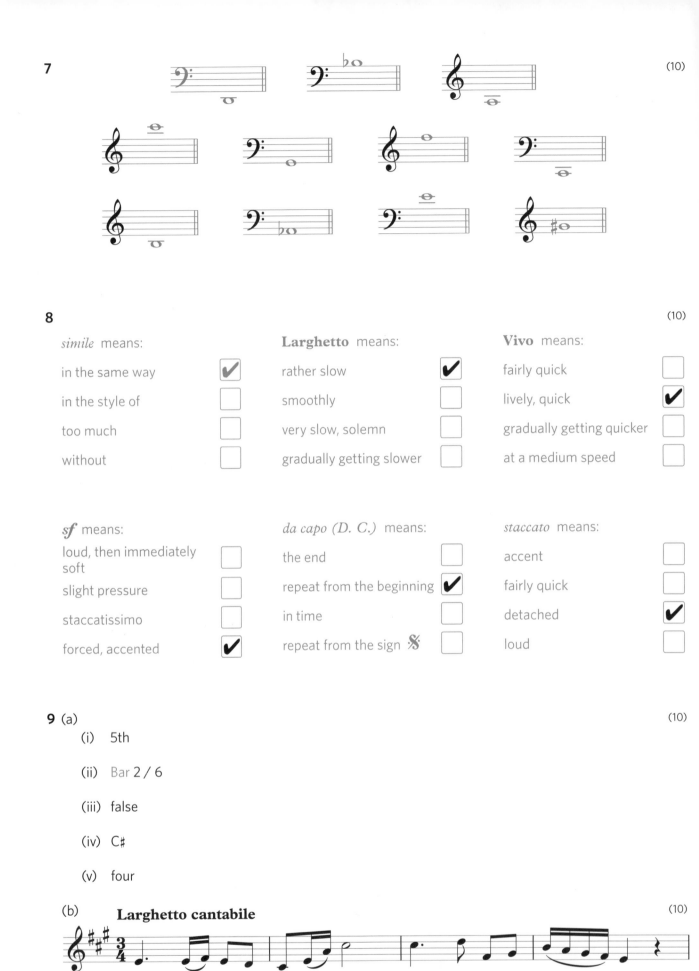

8 (10)

simile means:

in the same way ✔

in the style of ☐

too much ☐

without ☐

Larghetto means:

rather slow ✔

smoothly ☐

very slow, solemn ☐

gradually getting slower ☐

Vivo means:

fairly quick ☐

lively, quick ✔

gradually getting quicker ☐

at a medium speed ☐

sf means:

loud, then immediately soft ☐

slight pressure ☐

staccatissimo ☐

forced, accented ✔

da capo (D. C.) means:

the end ☐

repeat from the beginning ✔

in time ☐

repeat from the sign 𝄋 ☐

staccato means:

accent ☐

fairly quick ☐

detached ✔

loud ☐

9 (a) (10)

(i) 5th

(ii) Bar 2 / 6

(iii) false

(iv) C♯

(v) four

(b) **Larghetto cantabile** (10)

Theory Paper   Grade 2   2017   C
Model Answers

6   (10)

(a) G   A♭   B♭   C   G   E♭   C   F   D

(b) three

7   (10)

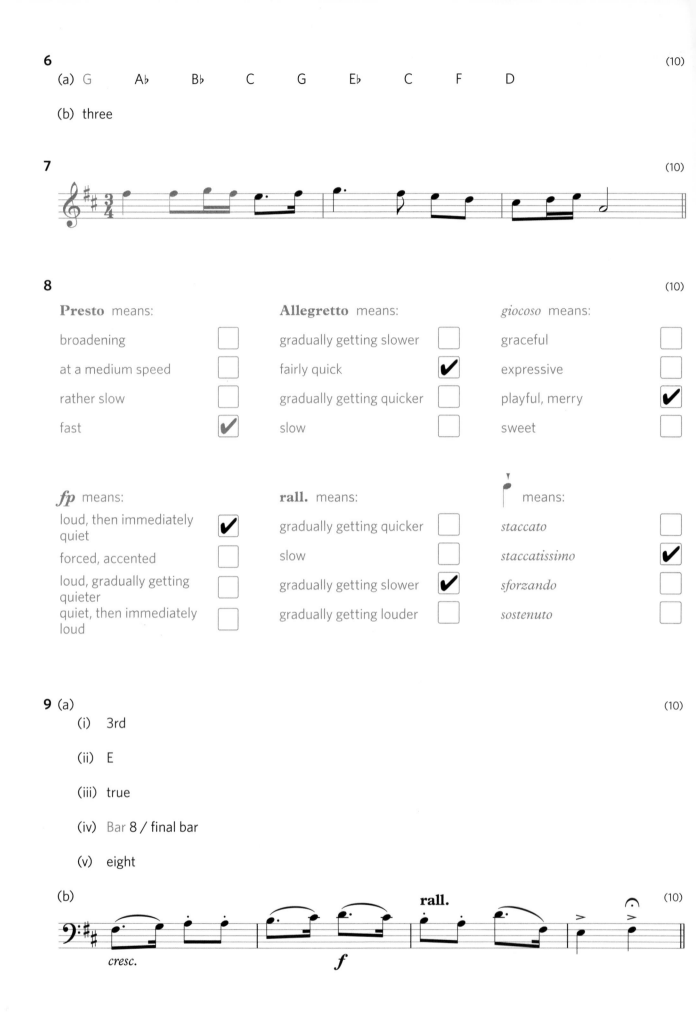

8   (10)

Presto means:

broadening ☐
at a medium speed ☐
rather slow ☐
fast ☑

Allegretto means:

gradually getting slower ☐
fairly quick ☑
gradually getting quicker ☐
slow ☐

giocoso means:

graceful ☐
expressive ☐
playful, merry ☑
sweet ☐

fp means:

loud, then immediately quiet ☑
forced, accented ☐
loud, gradually getting quieter ☐
quiet, then immediately loud ☐

rall. means:

gradually getting quicker ☐
slow ☐
gradually getting slower ☑
gradually getting louder ☐

means:

staccato ☐
staccatissimo ☑
sforzando ☐
sostenuto ☐

9 (a)   (10)

(i)   3rd

(ii) E

(iii) true

(iv) Bar 8 / final bar

(v)   eight

(b)   (10)

Theory Paper   Grade 2   2017   S
Model Answers

1   (10)

2   (10)

(a) 6th   4th   2nd   7th   6th   5th   3rd   1st /   8th /
                                                                                                                8th / 8ve   8ve / 1st

(b) four

3   (10)

4   (10)

5   (10)

harmonic   /   melodic

                                                                                            or

                                                                                            or

6 (10)

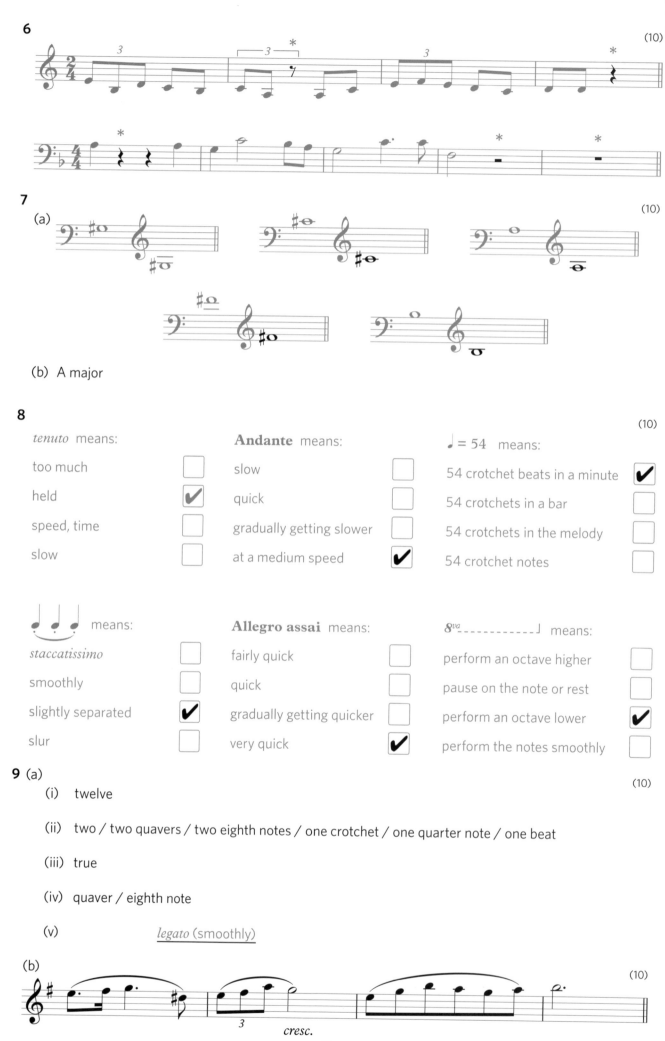

7 (10)

(a)

(b) A major

8 (10)

tenuto means:

- too much ☐
- held ☑
- speed, time ☐
- slow ☐

Andante means:

- slow ☐
- quick ☐
- gradually getting slower ☐
- at a medium speed ☑

♩ = 54 means:

- 54 crotchet beats in a minute ☑
- 54 crotchets in a bar ☐
- 54 crotchets in the melody ☐
- 54 crotchet notes ☐

means:

- *staccatissimo* ☐
- smoothly ☐
- slightly separated ☑
- slur ☐

Allegro assai means:

- fairly quick ☐
- quick ☐
- gradually getting quicker ☐
- very quick ☑

8ᵛᵃ- - - - - - - - ⌐ means:

- perform an octave higher ☐
- pause on the note or rest ☐
- perform an octave lower ☑
- perform the notes smoothly ☐

9 (a) (10)

(i) twelve

(ii) two / two quavers / two eighth notes / one crotchet / one quarter note / one beat

(iii) true

(iv) quaver / eighth note

(v) *legato* (smoothly)

(b) (10)

cresc.

Music Theory Practice Papers 2017 Model Answers

Model answers for four practice papers, adapted from ABRSM's 2017 Music Theory exams for Grade 2

Key features:

- a list of correct answers where appropriate
- a selection of likely options where the answer can be expressed in a variety of ways
- reflects the new question types in use from 2018

Support material for ABRSM Music Theory exams

**Supporting the teaching and learning of music
in partnership with the Royal Schools of Music**

Royal Academy of Music | Royal College of Music
Royal Northern College of Music | Royal Conservatoire of Scotland

www.abrsm.org f facebook.com/abrsm
 @abrsm   ABRSM YouTube

ISBN 978-1-78601-010-0